SEXciting
PUNography

Also by Harvey C. Gordon

PUNishment
The Art of Punning or How to Lose Friends
and Agonize People, 2nd ed.
(Warner Books, Inc.)

Grime and PUNishment
A Collection of Sexciting Puns
(Warner Books, Inc.)

PUNdemonium
Puns Are Everywhere!
(The Punster's Press*)

Baby Power
A Book about the Indignities of Babyhood
(The Punster's Press*)

*Distributed by Contemporary Books, Chicago

SEXciting PUNography

The Best Collection of Puns about Sex

A new, revised second edition of
Grime and PUNishment

She: Would you like one of my apples?
He: No, but I'm interested in your pair.

HARVEY C. GORDON

Illustrations by Frank Coronado

The Punster's Press
Publisher

The Punster's Press
Publisher

The Punster's Press, Publisher
2639 Maple Avenue
Northbrook, IL 60062

Library of Congress Control Number: 2016962911

ISBN: 978-0-9601402-0-6
ISBN eBook: 978-0-9601402-3-7

*I once again dedicate this book **to my jock strap***
for all the support it has given me through the years

CONTENTS

PREFACE

My second book, *Grime and PUNishment—A Collection of Sexciting Puns,* was published by Warner Books, Inc. (Time Warner, New York)* in 1981. As I stated in the Preface to the book, since my first pun book, *PUNishment—The Art of Punning or How to Lose Friends and Agonize People,* was a clean, general audience book, I could not call it "Grime and PUNishment", and consequently I remedied that situation when I chose "Grime and PUNishment" as the title for my second book of off-color, adult puns.

However, in the course of promoting *Grime and PUNishment,* including my 1981 book tour across the United States and Canada sponsored by Warner Books, I found that a number of people were mistakenly calling the book "Crime and PUNishment" (and were trying to find it under "C" in bookstores). That confusion is

---

* Now, Grand Central Publishing, a part of the Hachette Book Group

one reason I decided to change the title of the book to *SEXciting PUNography*. In addition, I changed the subtitle to *The Best Collection of Puns about Sex* because this new edition is the best collection of sex puns.

I also changed the title because I believe references to "grime" and "dirt" are now outdated. The puns in this new edition are off-color, sexual humor for adults; they are spicy, provocative and arousing, but not the product of a "dirty mind" or the result of "being naughty". Times have changed and off-color humor has become more mainstream and commonplace (although it might not be appropriate in every situation). The title "SEXciting PUNography" is more consistent with today's morality.

When I appeared on TV and radio programs during my book tour and when I did interviews for feature articles in major publications, I could not use most of the material from *Grime and PUNishment*. As a result, I ended up using a lot of material from *PUNishment* for the shows and interviews (as I did when I went on my first Warner-sponsored, cross-country tour for *PUNishment* in 1980). Fortunately, there are fewer media restrictions on adult humor today, and I am able to take advantage of the exposure provided by electronic media to publicize the new edition.

The new edition I have created is a revised, much improved version of the original *Grime and PUNishment* edition. I have added a substantial amount of new material, revised and updated a good portion of the material from the original book, and deleted a small amount of the original material (including a few illustrations), which I no longer consider "SEXciting" enough.

I have also divided the collection of puns in the new edition into nine categories, based on subject matter (e.g. The Oldest Profession—Female Prostitutes/ Call Girls) rather than just into the "Sexciting" and "X–Citing" categories I used in the original edition. I thought it would be more fun to allocate the puns in this manner plus the division into "Sexciting" and "X–citing" was pretty subjective. However, I should point out that the division of the new collection into subject matter categories is also not an exact science. Many puns in the collection could be placed into more than one category; for each of those puns, I picked the category that seemed to fit the best.

As I previously stated, since the art of punning is a highly creative activity, this book will go a long way toward promoting the art by tapping into one of the greatest of all creative resources—male and female sexual desires and their thoughts and fantasies about sex. The book should stimulate a large number of punsters by exposing them to an enjoyable and appealing source of new material. People who might not otherwise be interested in punning will have a chance to appreciate puns because of the SEXcitable nature of the book. Hopefully, even avowed abstainers will be enticed.

As with the original edition of the book, a number of the puns in the new edition are illustrated. However, again, because of my concern that the color would be off for illustrations of off-color puns, I had most of the drawings done in black and white. In creating the illustrations, my artist tried to em-barr-ass as few persons as possible.

In my book *PUNishment* I emphasized what makes punning an art is the ability to blend puns smoothly into normal conversation and the knack of creating clever puns spontaneously in appropriate situations.* When

---

* I have included an Appendix, entitled "Techniques for Punsters", at the end of the book, which discusses the techniques that can be used for blending puns smoothly into everyday conversation and creating puns spontaneously in certain situations. The Appendix is a slightly revised reproduction of Chapter 23, "Techniques for Punsters", from *PUNishment—The Art of Punning or How to Lose Friends and Agonize People, 2nd ed.* (New York: Warner Books, 1980), pp. 107–120.

presenting off-color puns at opportune moments, a punster must be sure to keep his composure and strive to be an artist in spite of the high degree of SEXcitement that can be aroused by the occasion.

I know there are some puns in my collection that are not politically correct by today's standards. However, it was not my intention in writing the book to be chauvinistic or condescending toward either sex nor do I, in any way, condone sexual harassment in the workplace or anywhere else. My goal was simply to come up with as many good, SEXciting puns as possible and use any format and wording that would express them effectively.

I believe I have added a substantial degree of new SEXcitement to this edition of the book. Hopefully, readers will enjoy my collection of sex puns and encourage many others to share their enjoyment. I just want to forewarn the reader, however, that trying to read *SEXciting PUNography* all at one time (instead of in multiple sittings) could result in a potent overdose of SEXciting humor, from which it might take a long time to recover.

Chapter 1

THE OLDEST PROFESSION—
FEMALE PROSTITUTES/
CALL GIRLS

– A number of call girls have been recruited by the CIA. They work as undercover agents.

– There is a high-priced prostitute staying at a classy hotel in New York who charges one thousand dollars a night for her services. The hotel refers to her suite as "The Grand Ballroom."

– There is a local escort service that arranges call girls in different cities for traveling businessmen. They call the arrangement their layaway plan.

– A couple of hookers were hired for a stag poker party to raise the men between their hands.

– A call girl in Dallas was once entertaining a young cowboy from a small west Texas town and was quite impressed with the young man's sexual sophistication. "I see you're no stranger to these parts, sonny," the woman acknowledged.

– A number of prostitutes are apathetic about voting in elections. They don't care who gets in.

– There is a lady of the evening who follows the fleet to a number of European ports. When asked why she travels so much to entertain sailors, she replied, "I really go for semen."

– A call girl once told a friend about a well-endowed man who always paid her with silver dollars. She referred to him as "Long John Silver."

– Many girls who work in brothels eventually take up long distance swimming. They're used to one lap after another.

– There is a prostitute living near an airport in New York who entertains a number of pilots. Her source of income is often referred to as "the cockpit."

– In the Old West, there was a room in a brothel that was occupied by an enthusiastic, heavyset woman who caused painful experiences for many of her customers. The room was often referred to as "The Nutcracker Suite."

– Ten minutes after finishing her sentence for prostitution, a hooker unknowingly solicited an undercover policeman on the street and was taken back into custody. Her second arrest illustrates the rule that one should never end a sentence with a proposition.

– I understand that most prostitutes calculate their annual income on December 31ˢᵗ. It's the end of their physical year.

– Many former hookers go to work for the IRS. They know all about internal revenue.

– After having the same two prostitutes brought before him for the third time, the irritated judge said, "You ladies are not getting the point even though it's been pounded into you over and over."

– Most prostitutes do not care about a customer's name. They think of him as John Dough.

– Apparently, some ladies of the evening make less than the minimum wage. I overhead one woman say that on a good night she can make three bucks an hour.

– I guess you've heard about the unfortunate Japanese call girl; no one had a yen for her.

– I heard about a prostitute who has a strong preference for chubby men; apparently, she believes in living off the fat of the land.

– Sometimes life for a prostitute can be a real grind.

– You might describe a call girl who is booked most days of the week as a busybody.

– I heard about a disappointed call girl who called all of her customers "John" for short because she never knew anyone too long.

– A woman who had been working in a brothel for many years was offered a job by an overnight delivery company. The company knew the woman could handle a package.

– There is a Nevada house of prostitution with a sign by its front door that reads: "Give our staff a chance to satisfy yours."

– Many hookers believe in astrology. They read their whore-a-scope every day.

– A number of magicians will hire former prostitutes as assistants. They already know how to do tricks.

– An enterprising hooker bought a bicycle and peddled it all over town.

– Tiny prostitutes have a tendency to sell themselves short.

– The ideal position for a prostitute on a women's touch football team would be wide receiver.

– Former hookers should never be hired to be home plate umpires in baseball. They're not used to keeping track of balls.

– Two hookers were once comparing notes and jokingly suggested that they inform the local Health Department about the epidemic of small cox in the area.

– A south Florida newspaper wanted to do a story about prostitutes in the Miami-Fort Lauderdale area during the tourist season. A punster editor suggested that a good title for the story might be "The Tail of Two Cities."

– A couple of successful prostitutes bought a large ranch in Nevada to use as their place of business. Their first customer was a rancher from Texas who told one of the ladies before he left, "Ma'am, you have quite a nice spread out here."

– A businessman phoned a call girl upon arriving in town and asked, "Are you free tonight?" "No," the woman replied, "but I'm reasonable."

– An enterprising lady of the evening could refer to her source of income as "The Chamber of Commerce."

– There is a part-time dancer in Las Vegas who makes big money as a call girl when she's not filling in at one end of the chorus line or the other. In other words, some nights she dances on her right leg, other nights she dances on her left leg, and in between she makes a nice living.

– A young newspaper reporter, doing a story about a Nevada brothel, asked a long-time employee who always walks around the brothel in a bath robe, whether anything was worn under her robe. The woman replied, "Nope. Everything's as good as it ever was".

– I heard about a prostitute who keeps a diary of all her experiences. She once made an entry about an eighty-year-old patron that read: "He's the oldest trick in the book ...."

– A brothel employee helped a prostitute steal a sizable amount of money from one of her clients while the man was having sex with her. The police considered the theft to be an inside job.

– Most hookers put in long hours. They work around the cock.

– In biblical times some enterprising prostitutes tried to make a prophet.

– A prostitute at a brothel came up to a new, young client in the waiting room and said "Honey, why don't we have a little talk…." She then sat on his lap seductively and continued, "And we can see what pops up".

– A businessman, who was planning an upcoming trip, called his favorite call girl and asked "How's your schedule next week", to which the woman replied "Honey, I'm wide open".

Chapter 2

PENAL MATTERS—
HIS BODY/MALE PROSTITUTES
AND STRIPPERS

– A man had a $100 bill tattooed on his penis for the following reasons: so he could play with his money; so he could watch his money grow; and, if his wife ever wanted to blow a hundred bucks, he could tell her where to go.

– When a male stripper became tired of his profession and was ready to quit, his boss persuaded him to stick it out a little longer.

– Throughout history, many disappointed wives of kings and dictators have discovered that not every ruler has twelve inches.

– A couple was becoming quite frustrated over the man's prolonged period of impotency and decided to seek professional help. After three sessions of sexual therapy, the matter was brought to a head.

– Two sorority girls went away for an intimate ski weekend with their boyfriends. The day they arrived at the ski lodge, they texted their sorority sister that there wasn't any snow yet, but they were expecting six or seven inches that night.

– Since in Pharmacology all drugs have both a trade name and a generic name, the FDA is rumored to be looking for a generic name for Viagra; names rumored to be under consideration are "Mycoxafloppin", "Mycoxa-failin", "Mydixadrupin", "Mydixarizin" and "Ibepokin".

– A high school freshman had some of his friends come over to watch some porn he found in his older brother's room. By the end of the film, there wasn't a dry fly in the house.

– A man got drunk at a party and started stripping down to his underwear while doing a wild, erotic dance. You might say the man was doing a takeoff of a male stripper.

— Rumor has it that a major beverage company will be using liquid Viagra for a new energy beverage that also can serve as a drink mixer. They won't be able to call the beverage a "soft drink", and as a mixer, it will give new meaning to the words "cocktail" and "stiff drink". Allegedly, the name for the new beverage will be "MOUNT & DO".

— A roller skate manufacturer and an athletic supporter company recently decided to merge because they were both familiar with ball-bearing items.

– Gigolos achieve success in an unconventional way. They start on top and work their way down.

– I know a chauffeur who played strip poker last night for the first time. He learned that the more you lose, the more you have to show for it.

– I know a woman who has a foot fetish. She only makes it with well-endowed men.

– I understand that a "condominium" is nothing more than a prophylactic for a small person.

– A wealthy hermit who has not been with a woman in ten years considers himself to be a self-made man.

– To satisfy some older women, a male prostitute will have to put in overtime. (Eventually, however, he will peter out.)

– When an attractive young nurse told her male patient that she needed to "prick his finger" to get a blood sample, the smiling man replied, "I'd rather have you finger my prick".

– I understand that a sexologist is writing an article about the male reproductive organ after climax; he would like to call it "Withering Heights."

– A little person was thrown out of a nudist camp for sticking his nose in other people's business.

– A couple of women joined a strip poker game with a group of men and managed to raise them a number of times.

– A number of men who want to make it with the ladies soak themselves in an ice-cold bath water before going out. They realize that cooler heads will prevail.

– Experienced women know that the first thing to come out of the male organ during lovemaking is the wrinkles.

– A sergeant and two good looking men from his platoon went to a tavern near the base one night. When the sergeant asked an attractive army nurse to join him in a game of pool, the nurse said she would rather play with his privates.

– Sexologists have learned that Native Americans living along the northern Pacific coast often refer to their erections as scrotum poles.

– You might describe male prostitutes as working stiffs.

– There is a special bakery in San Francisco that makes cookies in the shape of the male reproductive organ. The cookies are sold with doughnuts, and the bakery refers to the cookie sheet it uses as its "peter pan". (You might say the bakers knead to make women happy.)

– A woman was talking to a guy and admiring the nice sportswear he had bought at Dick's Sporting Goods. When the woman said "Unfortunately, we don't have Dick's in our town", the guy replied "That must be tough on you ladies".

– A man living in Utah has seven wives. On most days, six of them have it pretty soft.

– Years ago, before internet porn, a man walked into a porno movie theater wearing nothing but shoes, socks, and a raincoat. When the usherette at the door asked to see his ticket, the man opened his coat and exposed himself. The woman calmly replied, "I asked to see your ticket—not your stub."

– Even after studying about the male reproductive organ in their sex education classes, a number of high school girls are still unable to grasp the subject.

– Gardeners have trouble explaining how the male organ can be fully grown before planted.

– A number of years ago a friend of mine picked up his date and told her they were going to see the movie *Papillion*—a film about a French penal colony. His date shyly inquired whether the movie was about an all-male nudist camp.

– Many years ago a male prostitute sent a note to a prospective client that read "Do you want to see something swell".

Chapter 3
"T" & "A"—HER BODY/FEMALE STRIPPERS AND DANCERS

– A store in Las Vegas that sells swimwear for women has a special section for bikinis with easily-removable tops; the section is called "Off the Rack".

– A female human resource executive became very embarrassed when she was interviewing a male job applicant and asked her assistant, "Do I have an opening this man will fit?"

– A woman who was taking driving lessons with a male instructor became very upset when she was backing out of a diagonal parking space with an obstructed view and he told her to gradually expose her rear end.

– I used to go out with a girl whose kissing left something to be desired—the rest of her body.

– Eating places like Hooters and Twin Peaks, with well-endowed, attractive servers, are often referred to as "breastaurants".

– A man and a woman met each other while sitting at a bar. After a while the man said, "If I have one more drink, I'll start to feel it," to which the woman replied, "If I have one more, I'll let you."

– There is a woman who likes lifting her shirt up and shinning a portable light on her boobs at nighttime beach parties. She refers to the light as her flash-light.

– In response to a friend inquiring why he was so upset about a female co-worker leaving his company, the man simply said "harassment". When his puzzled friend timidly asked if he sexually harassed her, the man said "No. I used to sit behind her and "her ass meant" everything to me".

– An attractive English lawyer named Esther, who was working as a solicitor in London, decided to take a part-time job as a stripper at a nightclub in town. She wanted to be a bare Esther (barrister).*

---

*A barrister is a qualified member of the legal profession in England who presents and pleads cases in superior court while a solicitor is not a member of the bar and may not plead cases in superior court.

– Female billiard players routinely wear push-up bras when they play. They like to rack 'em up.

– When I was in Hawaii, I saw a beautiful display of hula dancing; you might say that hula dancing is an asset to Hawaiian music.

– An Australian celebrity wore a very revealing open weave top to show off her large, pendulous breasts. Her boobs were definitely Down Under.

– A woman had a breast enlargement operation and was delighted with the results. She wrote a special note to her doctor that read: "Thanks for the Mammaries."

– A well-endowed country singer was escorted off the stage by a good-looking male singer at an awards ceremony. The host inadvertently commented: "They're a lovely pair".

– After auditioning in a bikini for a part in a commercial, a voluptuous girl leaned over and told the man in charge, "If you're interested, you know where to get a hold of me.

– I understand that the person who created the miniskirt was a sex enthusiast named Seymour Butz. (I wonder what he's up to now.)

– A well-endowed woman who could only support herself by working as a topless dancer was once chastised about her profession. "Well," she replied sadly, "it's better than being flat busted."

– A businesswoman in a low-cut dress attended a meeting with a number of men and felt very insecure. It seemed that everyone was looking down on her.

– Some male bosses will not hire a female secretary or receptionist until they have checked out her legs. Other bosses are above that.

– I heard about a salesman who sells padded bras from door to door. Women refer to him as the fuller bust man. (I understand that whenever he goes out selling, he wears his best duds.)

– In an attempt to seduce a good-looking college grad, an older, well-endowed woman sat next to him on the couch, engaged in seductive small talk and eventually leaned his head onto her breasts. For the college grad, it was a tit-illating conversation.

– There is an administrative assistant who has been pregnant so many times that whenever she types a letter on her computer, she automatically skips two consecutive periods.

– A famous Las Vegas hotel has a special suite for a well-endowed female entertainer who often performs at the hotel's nightclub. The suite has no doorbell—just two knockers.

– A friend of mine told me he reads *Playboy* and *Penthouse* for the same reason he reads *National Geographic*—to see beautiful places he will never visit.

– A former Miss America was running for Congress. In discussing her successful fund raising, a newscaster said, "She has quite a campaign chest."

– A topless dancer was told by her boss that she would get twice as much money if she danced bottomless and there were no strings attached.

– A man decided to ask the baker's shapely assistant out because he liked her buns.

– Initially, the teenage girl was able to keep her pregnancy a secret from her friends; however, months later her situation became apparent.

– A man walked into his doctor's office and said to the shapely receptionist, "If I told you that you had a great body, would you hold it against me?"

– When a well-endowed country singer fainted on stage, it took six men to carry her off—three abreast.

– A topless female band can have a lot of sax appeal.

– A shapely farm girl was selling apples at the State Fair when a young man approached her stand. "Sir, would you like one of my apples?" "No," the man replied, "but I'm interested in your pair."

– A well-endowed young woman wore a bikini with a push-up top in a beauty contest. She stacked up well against the competition.

– I heard about a woman who has been involved with a number of players on the New York Jets. Her boobs are now referred to as "The Jet Set."

– A well-endowed lady who was speaking at a celebrity roast was flanked by two male TV stars. She said, "Who ever thought I would be standing here with two biggies."

– You might say that silicone injections are the answer to a maiden's pair.

– I understand that some women who have to walk alone at night attach mousetrap-type gadgets to their bras in case they are attacked. These innovative devices might be called "booby traps."

– Last night I went to a topless bar and saw impressive pole dancing by a very well-endowed young woman. The dancer was outstanding.

– To the men who watch them, striptease dancers are girls with appeal.

– A striptease dancer was doing her thing on stage when the theater curtains fell and completely engulfed her. The dancer threw off the curtains and yelled, "I've been draped."

– I was told that many players on the Pittsburgh Pirates like to go out with women with boyish figures. This preference is not surprising since a pirate's dream has always been a sunken chest.

– A shapely college girl who had not seen her boyfriend all summer threw herself into his arms and said, "Hug me until I break!" Her boyfriend squeezed her until he felt her crack.

– A womanizing buyer for ladies' clothes, pretending to be interested in the fabric an attractive model was wearing, pinched some material from her dress near her breasts and said, "Can this be felt?"

– A topless dancer who gets men excited with her body might think of her boobs as an erector set.

– A recent survey by a women's magazine found that women who wear heavily-padded bras overwhelmingly like the same brand of candy: Milk Duds.

A friend of mine used to read his news magazines every week. Now he spends his time reading various men's magazines instead. You might say he has been getting a little behind in his reading.

– A bra-less woman with a great body wanted to show off and have some fun with a group of men. She lifted up her shirt, but then pulled it right down again quickly. You might say her boobs were gone in a flash.

Chapter 4

AFFAIRS, FOOLING AROUND AND WORKPLACE SEXCAPADES

– A man's female boss was requiring him to work very late night after night. He was having a hard time with it, and complained to a friend that his boss was really riding him lately.

– A hotel with deluxe banquet facilities caused a number of auto mishaps in an affluent California community when it put up a roadside sign that read: "Have Your Next Affair Here".

– Many Congressmen are very adaptable in their relationships with their female interns. They're always turning a new page.

– I know a guy who often fools around with his secretary at the office. When he does, he goes home and tells his wife he had a hard day at the office.

– A man was confronted by his wife about his involvement with another woman and confessed to having a second marriage in another state. When his wife reacted with disbelief, the man said, "I think it was bigamy to admit it."

– I understand that many chess players have love affairs in The Czech Republic. They love Czech mates.

– One business executive we know allows his promiscuous secretary to schedule all his appointments because he knows she's great on dates.

– A member of the faculty orientation committee was summoned to the Chancellor's office after allegedly fooling around with one of the female students during orientation week. His defense was that he was just getting to know the student body.

– A male Olympic swimming coach kept a shapely girl on the team even though she was not one of the best swimmers. Apparently, he liked her strokes.

– An attractive female lobbyist in Washington denied providing Congressmen with sexual favors for votes on a tit-for-tat basis.

– At the office Christmas party everyone was feeling merry, so she left.

– I know a man who was married to a woman named Edith and having a glorious affair with a young girl named Kate. His wife found out about the affair and divorced him immediately, which only goes to show you that you can't have your Kate and Edith too.

– Did you hear about the man on the flying trapeze who caught his wife in the act?

– A businessman first told his secretary to buy herself a new dress for her birthday. Then he tried to talk her out of it.

– Some high school teachers have affairs with their fellow faculty members while others stick to their principals.

– A woman entertained a lover while her husband was working late and was not careful about protecting her bedsheets. When her husband was getting into bed that night, she smiled at him but he looked at her with disdain.

– A receptionist was excited about the prospects at her new job. Her boss told her there would be many opportunities for advances.

– A male and female optometrist who share the same office suite were grinding away together in the office one day and made a spectacle of themselves.

– For female employees, wild Christmas parties can become an ass-felt jungle.

– Upon hiring a young, attractive female attorney, the lecherous senior partner of a law firm told her to get some experience under her belt and always try to get ahead, even when it's hard.

– A corporate executive was constantly pinching his receptionist at the office. His aim was to harass.

– My neighbor's wife came home unexpectedly one day and found him in bed with another woman; the man was scared stiff.

– A businessman who liked to pat his female employees on the fanny was warned by the women that they would file a sexual harassment complaint if he touched them again, and there were to be no ifs, ands, or butts.

– A woman who has been going out with a married man for six months is not sure where the relationship is going. She's been kept in the dark.

– Some women have trouble working for a woman boss. They're used to having a man over them.

– A lawyer and his secretary were at the office late one evening allegedly to organize files and straighten his office. The lawyer's wife happened to stop by the office and found the secretary going through her husband's drawers.

– A woman who found out her husband was living with two other women in different states lost control and cut off his penis. You might say she's crazy and he's just nuts.

– A man who was having sex with his assistant after hours in his office had her bind his hands together as part of a sexual fantasy. When a text came in from his wife, asking why he wasn't home yet, he told his assistant to reply that he was tied up at the office.

– When a woman was no longer able to reach sexual climax with her boyfriend, she decided to seduce a good-looking man in her office and try him on for sighs.

– A photographer's assistant was madly in love with her boss and anxious to get him alone in the dark. One afternoon while her boss was making blow-ups of some of her negatives, she decided to join him in the darkroom and help him enlarge.

– The owner of a flower shop asked his shapely young assistant to stay late one night and help him inventory and rearrange all of the store's merchandise. When the man's wife dropped by the shop around ten, she caught her husband with his plants down.

– A female lawyer in the JAG Corps decided to have a one night stand with a military judge in her department just before leaving the Army. Apparently, she wanted an Honor-able discharge.

– There is a radio station engineer who often has sex with his female colleagues at his work station. You might say he does it with frequency.

– Many international playboys have been recruited into our diplomatic service. They're well versed in foreign affairs.

Chapter 5
MAKING LOVE/INTERCOURSE/ HAVING SEX

– A man took out his tailor's daughter and spent a most enjoyable night with her. In the morning he told her that she was the only thing her father ever made that fit him.

– There's a woman with a number of lovers who routinely checks her emails during sex. She likes to keep track of the mail in her in-box.

– A well-known comedian once said that having sex is like playing bridge; if you don't have a good partner, you'd better have a good hand.

– A woman ended her relationship with a man who worked for a frozen orange juice company. During sex, the man couldn't concentrate.

– I know a promiscuous female stockbroker who makes sure that all her male clients get their share.

– A sex therapist once described the progressive effect of aging on a couple's sexual activity as "tri-weekly, try weekly, try weakly".

– In the middle of the night a man might compare his wife's body to a convenience store—there's not a lot of variety, but it's all that is open at 3:00 a.m.

– A promiscuous woman indiscriminately had sex with a number of different men without taking oral contraceptives. You might say she had no screw pills.

– A high school senior thought he had enough time to make love to his girlfriend in his room while his mother was making dinner. When his mother called him to eat sooner than expected, the boy yelled, "I'm coming!"

– My friend Paul has sex often with a number of women so whenever I phone him, I start out by saying: "Are you in the middle of someone". {A little bit of a stretch}

– A virgin college girl and ceramic floor tiles have one thing in common. It's important that they're laid properly the first time.

– After seeing the man's gorgeous voluptuous girlfriend and then hearing the man say he can never resist having sex with her, his friend said: "I can see where you're coming from". (It's obvious the man is addicted to having sex with the woman.)

– Some men do not sleep well on their honeymoon. They get up three or four times a night.

– During his evening security check, a bailiff entered a judge's chambers and unexpectedly found the judge making love to one of the court reporters. "Your Honor!" the startled bailiff exclaimed. "No, you fool," the annoyed judge replied, "she's on me."

– When told by his boss to start developing a life-size doll that could be used for sexual intercourse, the engineer replied, "I'll get right on it."

– Many farmer's daughters will only make it with city men because farm hands are too rough.

– An elderly gentleman was greatly concerned about being able to satisfy his lady friend during their first night together. Fortunately, he was able to rise to the occasion.

– During the Middle Ages a number of maidens sought comfort on long, lonely knights.

– A couple came home from a New Year's Eve party shortly after midnight to make love. They wanted to start the New Year off with a bang.

– Two married women were out having lunch together. One of the women told her companion an off-color joke she had heard recently, and when her friend did not crack a smile, she said, "Don't you get it?" Her companion replied, "Not very often."

– A number of younger men get religious during love-making. They often talk about the Second Coming.

– Many lovemaking sessions end with a gland finale.

– Some women compare sex with a new partner to an impending winter storm; they don't know how many inches they will get nor how long it will last.

– Some college girls have a faculty for making love; others just do it with fellow students.

– When at first the amorous coed could not convince her date to make love, she tried some genital persuasion.

– A guy and his girlfriend were parked and "going at it" in the front seat of his car. In the heat of passion, the eager lover repeatedly hit the steering wheel horn with his body. After several honks, the girl finally said, "I didn't realize you were so horny."

– A woman was romantically involved with her dentist and planning to stay overnight at his apartment. She told him not to forget to cap it when he proceeds with the inlay.

– A social-climbing American woman took advantage of her trip to Europe to meet and pursue some of the continent's most prominent noblemen. She managed to make every second count.

When a world-renowned bridge player was asked what he would do if he held the queen alone, he replied, "Take her to bed until the king was expected home".

– When a college man told his girlfriend that the time was right for them to make love, she replied, "I'm with you every inch of the way."

– A teller at a local bank who enjoys flirting with the bank's customers recently became pregnant. Apparently, someone made a very special deposit.

– After tying her lover's hands to the bed posts as part of a bondage fantasy, a woman was surprised when the man wrapped his arms around her passionately. When the woman said "I thought I had you tied down", the smiling man replied "frayed knot".

– A young married couple decided to seek counseling about their deteriorating sex life, which was attributable to their mutual desire to be on top during lovemaking. They told the therapist that the problem was mounting.

– A man went into a bank to purchase a Certificate of Deposit and hit it off with the new accounts lady. After going out a few times and becoming physically involved, the lady decided to end the relationship. When the man asked why she was breaking things off, she replied, "As I told you at the bank, early withdrawal results in loss of interest."

– Have you heard about the young lovers who didn't fall asleep until after three?

– A woman brought a paternity suit against her psychologist. Apparently, when sex was discussed during their therapy sessions, the woman was quite open.

– A smooth-talking ladies' man who was hitchhiking through the French countryside was able to persuade a number of country girls to join him in the hayloft. You might say that the man is for whom the belles roll.

– An American college student on a tour of Finland was able to use his limited Finnish vocabulary to persuade a pretty native girl to spend the night with him. Upon departing for Sweden the next morning, the man apologized for his lack of familiarity with the girl's language by saying, "I'm afraid my Finnish isn't too good," to which the girl responded, "Neither is your foreplay."

– A dentist was accused of taking sexual liberties with one of his patients while she was under sedation. When the woman's attorney requested access to her dental file, he was told that it could not be found. The attorney replied, "The file isn't the only thing that's been mislaid.

– A coed and her boyfriend from the state university decided to check into a motel for the five days between their winter and spring courses. You might describe this part of their curriculum as "intercourse."

– A middle-aged man who was depressed because he was aging had a number of one-night stands with younger women; however, each affair only added to his severe depression. You might say the man was falling apart piece by piece.

– I heard about an elderly gentleman who went to bed with a lady friend at two in the afternoon and didn't get up until five.

– A girl was somewhat disappointed with her first sexual experience. She told one of her friends, "It was no big thing."

– A couple went to a therapist about a sexual problem involving the husband's dislike for the dominant position during intercourse. After a few sessions, the parties were optimistic about resolving the issue; they agreed that the problem was "Sir Mountable."

– When at first the unpassionate lady's man was unable to seduce his date, he tried a little ardor.

– A friend of mine told me that on his last trip to Paris he met and became friendly with an attractive French girl. The first night he made love to her in his hotel room he recalls her saying "Je t'adore" over and over, and he kept replying, "It's closed, it's closed".

– A judge's wife told her husband that his preoccupation with work was ruining their sex life. He was just going through the motions.

– When a woman suggested that her partner start taking Viagra to make their lovemaking better, the man said he was definitely up for it.

– Recently, when it comes to women, I would say the word "connoisseur" applies to my friend Louie. He shacked up with two beautiful women over the weekend and is now "kinda sore" from it. {Another stretch}

– Men who get too drunk on their wedding night end up doing things half-cocked.

– I read about an innkeeper's daughter during the Middle Ages who made love for fifteen straight knights.

– When her parents went out of town, a high school girl let her boyfriend spend the night with her; however, she would not admit it.

– A postman stopped at his girlfriend's house for a quickie before starting his morning rounds. You might say the lady received her male early that morning.

– When a newly married woman told her girlfriend that married life with her husband was a pain in the ass, her girlfriend replied "he's missing the target".

– A well-known comedian was bleeped on a late-night talk show when the host asked him what he wanted most in a woman and he replied, "About seven or eight inches."

– A sixty-year-old man had to give up sex with his wife for a few months because of a prostate operation. However, now he is back in the groove.

– Most dentists turn out to be great lovers. They're used to drilling cavities.

– A dejected man who was afraid of losing his masculinity with age had an affair with a much younger woman to boost his spirits. However, the affair did not help his state of mind. When the woman wanted to make love twice in a row, the man realized he was too depressed. (A number of midlife-crisis men believe that making love to an attractive younger woman will give them a lift.)

– Some female nurses can make a bed without disturbing the patient; others can make the patient without disturbing the bed.

– In the business world, an aggressive woman who will not take things lying down can end up in the top position.

– Some men will make love to any woman whatsoever at any time, if she's willing to be on top. You might say they're always hard up.

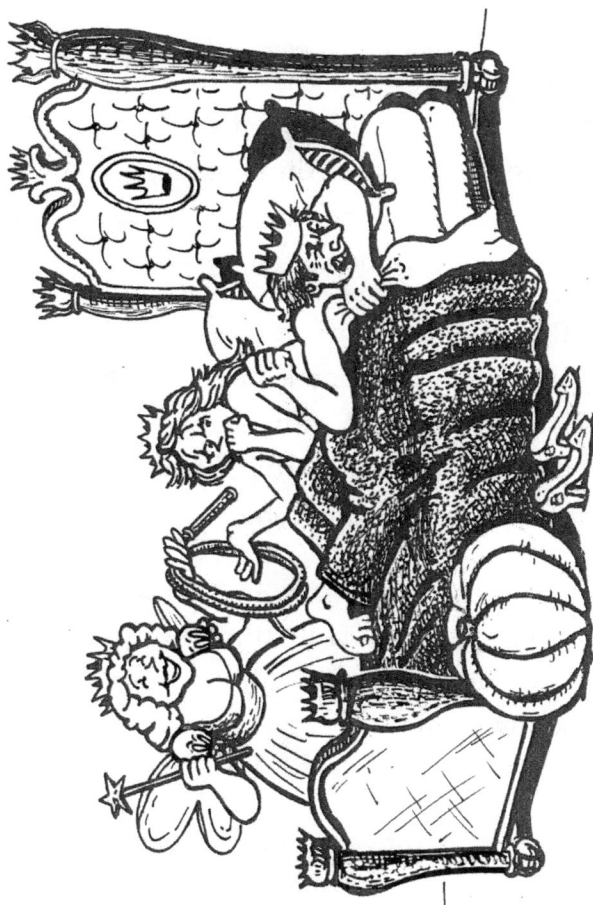

I understand they have made an X-rated movie sequel to the Cinderella story in which the Prince goes through a prolonged period of impotency, and Cinderella, after acting out a number of fantasies without success, wistfully sighs, "Someday my prince will come."

– A first year law student checked into a motel to study for his finals, but had his girlfriend stop by periodically for sex breaks. You could say the student was boning up for his exams.

– A marathon runner, who had been wearing a tight athletic supporter for the past three hours, asked his girlfriend to join him in the bedroom so he could slip into something more comfortable.

– A Human Resource department conducted its own investigation as to whether a male employee actually engaged in sexual intercourse with a female employee after the company's Christmas party. The HR manager considered it to be an internal probe.

– A politician during a recent election allegedly told some staff members that his incumbent opponent should only make love with his wife on top because he's used to screwing up.

– A man from the city drove to a suburban housing development and was shown a ranch model by one of the developer's sexy salesladies. After being alone in the house with the lady for over an hour, the man returned to the sales office and said, 'You have quite a nice lay out here."

– When getting ready for sex, the woman told her partner that she never likes being on top. The smiling man replied, "Get over it".

– A female espionage agent tried to seduce a man to get valuable information without knowing that the man was impotent. It turned out to be emission impossible.

– I know a promiscuous woman who often has uncontrollable crying spells. She's constantly bawling.

– In the heat of wild passion, a young couple started tearing each other's clothes off and making love in the bathroom. The passion was so great that even the shower got turned on.

– After meeting and hitting it off for hours on the dance floor, a woman whispered "I think we should hook up" in the man's ear during a slow dance. The man replied "I'm in".

– A woman who jumps from one man's bed to another could be considered a pole vaulter.

– There is a woman named Lisa who makes a great deal of moaning sounds during lovemaking. Her lovers refer to her as "Mona-Lisa".

– A girl at one of the local high schools thought she was entitled to a varsity letter for making the basketball team.

Chapter 6
NUDITY/STREAKING/NUDE MODELLING

– A man walked into a psychiatrist's office wearing nothing but cellophane wrap. The psychiatrist said "I can clearly see you're nuts".

– A group of male and female college students were planning to conduct a nude protest at the school's graduation ceremony. However, the women didn't have the balls to go through with it.

– A newspaper reported that someone drilled a hole in the wall surrounding a nudist camp on the outskirts of town. The police are looking into it.

– A nudist colony usually has a number of sunbathing buffs.

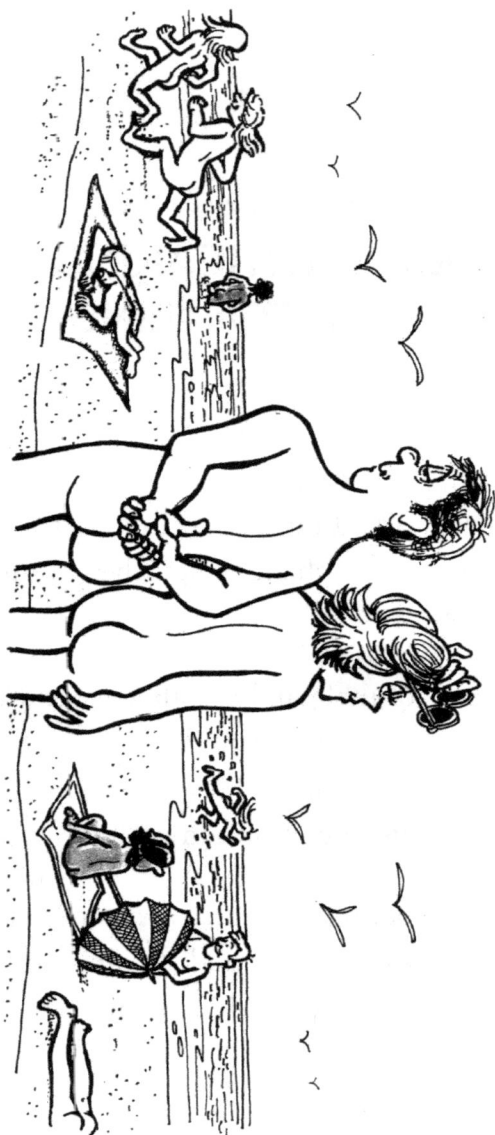

When I was in Maui, I visited a crowded nude beach where everyone was glancing cheek to cheek.

– A photographer interviewed a number of swimsuit models to pose for a men's magazine. Some of the girls were unsuited for the job.

– A lady invited a gentleman over to her house for dinner and a moonlight skinny dip in her private pool. To set the mood, the lady served strip steaks for dinner.

– The atmosphere at a nudist colony is very relaxed. The members let it all hang out.

– A sign was posted at the entrance to the nude beach I visited that read: "Please bare with us."

– I soon realized how nervous I was at the beach when I walked up to a lady to get change for a vending machine and asked if she had two nipples for a dime.

– A woman with a great body became a little shy upon arriving at a nude beach and decided to lay face down in the sand near a group of men. However, she thought she could still make a good impression.

– A couple of nudists who were dating each other exclusively for about six months recently decided to go out with other people. They felt they were seeing too much of each other.

– A visit to a nudist camp can be very therapeutic for a relationship. It's a good place for a man and woman to air their differences.

– A young lady only streaked topless across campus because a completely nude body was more than she could bare.

– The publisher of a horse-breeding magazine with declining circulation is planning to feature a topless woman on one of its prime young horses every month. This feature will be advertised as their monthly center foal. The publisher hopes it will stirrup some interest in the magazine.

– A modest woman who was vacationing at a dude ranch in Arizona was shocked when the riding instructor asked her if she wanted to ride bare back.

– A streaker once ran into a policewoman on the outskirts of the college campus; however, she was unable to pin anything on him.

– Two male vacationers gave up their plans to visit a nude beach after hearing the tour guide say that prolonged exposure to the tropical sun could result in prickly heat.

A young actor was advised by his agent to model nude for a women's magazine. The agent apparently felt his client needed the exposure.

– When a woman was asked if she would be able to find a missing blind man at a nude beach, she replied "It wouldn't be hard".

– A well-known Caribbean resort recently became a nudist retreat and the resort's apparel shop decided to have a clothes-out sale.

Chapter 7
ACTORS/ARTISTS
AND THE ARTS

– I understand there is a new British porn movie coming out soon with the title "Loins of London".

– Shortly after arriving in Hollywood, an attractive young actress got involved in successive love affairs with several leading screen actors. The woman always had a desire to make love under the stars.

– The director of a new pornographic movie auditioned a young actress to see if she could handle the part.

– An actor and actress who have made a number of porn flicks are now out of work. You might say that they are among the hardcore unemployed.

– A New York writer was offered an excellent opportunity to go to Hollywood and write for a popular TV show. However, the voluptuous woman he was living with did not want to move to the West Coast. For the writer, it was clearly a case of Hollywood or bust.

– Did you hear about the successful porn movie that grossed millions?

– A cheerleader for a professional football team lost her job after she posed naked in a pornographic movie. She'll now have to find a new position.

– An aspiring young actress decided to have silicone implants and rear end augmentation after she was told by a Broadway producer that before she could become a star, she would have to become a little meteor.

– After reviewing some of her film clips, a director decided not to hire a former porn star for a leading role in a new movie. Apparently, he did not like her parts.

– An attractive girl from the Midwest who wanted to be an actress more than anything moved to New York and enrolled in acting school. However, after struggling for a while, she decided it would be best for her to make her way into show business.

– A long time ago there was an obscene nightclub entertainer in Las Vegas who considered himself to be a band singer. His songs were banned in a number of states.

– I heard rumors that a new hardcore pornographic movie is in the works. The producers would like to use the title "The Pit and the Pendulum".

– An X-rated western is going to be released shortly. The wagons are the only things that will be covered.

– There is an artist who specializes in obscene oil portraits. His paint is made from crude oil.

– The increased amount of nudity in recent movies has appealed to film buffs.

– For some people the money made from hardcore porn movies might be described as gross profit.

– I understand that the American adult video industry lists new movies that are still in production in the "Coming Soon" category.

Chapter 8
SPORTS AND ATHLETES

– Many women do not enjoy having a basketball player for a lover because they usually dribble before they shoot.

– A basketball player thinks of lovemaking with the woman on top as a lay-up.

– Many women will not date a defensive lineman on a football team; all they have on their mind is sacks.

– A number of golfing couples have open marriages. They're real swingers.

– Apparently, some golfers work on their putting game after the sun goes down. A fellow once told me he made a five-footer under the moonlight.

– Rumor has it that after winning the championship game a number of years ago, a seven-foot basketball player walked right into his favorite bar and said, "The highballs are on me."

– Avid male golfers are not happy unless they make love to many women. They're used to 18 holes.

– At Wimbledon this year one of the female tennis players popped out of the top of her tennis dress while trying to return a low shot. You might say she had a falling out with the crowd.

– A cheerleader for a college football team decided to have a breast enlargement operation shortly before the first football game. It was the first two-point conversion of the season.

– I was told about a female cheerleader for the University of Minnesota football team who had a lot of school spirit. She would gopher any player on the team.

– A recent survey of coeds disclosed that football players who play wide out and slot receiver are the least desirable lovers on campus. Apparently, no girl wants you when you're down and out.

– A mixed doubles team at a singles resort did not hit it off well either on or off the court because he wanted to score and she wanted to end up with love.

– A female singles tennis star from the United States got pregnant while on tour in Europe. She is now playing doubles.

– At a singles bar, unlike in a football game, a field goal kicker can score with a near miss.

– Did you hear about the overly anxious baseball player who went for a fast ball, popped up, and couldn't score?

– A man and a woman met at a tennis club and decided to rally for a while. As they approached the court, the man asked, "Is that a new can?" The woman looked down over her shoulder and replied, "No; it's the same one I've always had."

– When a jockey picks up a girl who's "hot to trot", he'll take her to a hotel and check into the Bridal Suite. Some jockeys have a one-track mind.

– A superstitious professional golfer once told a sports magazine interviewer that he has his wife rub his balls for luck before a big tournament. It helps straighten his putts.

– Some pitchers have a lot in common with people who attend orgies. They both like screwballs.

– Supposedly, major league shortstops make great lovers. They're used to going deep in the hole.

Chapter 9
MISCELLANEOUS

– The police recently raided a massage parlor in our city. Evidently, a masseuse rubbed someone the wrong way.

– For years the most popular fraternity on all college campuses has been I Phelta Thi.

– A single guy's apartment should have some wide couches, a comfortable bed and one night stand.

– A recent survey by a men's magazine has disclosed that a young guy's favorite breakfast is a roll with some honey.

– There are a few social ultraconservatives who think transgender men should be arrested for male fraud.

– You can always tell that you're at a male homosexual bar by the gaze in everyone's eyes.

– A man on a business trip went to a singles bar, approached two ladies, and offered either of them a hundred dollars to spend the night with him. One lady stormed out in a rage, but the other remained cool, calm and collected.

– Sexually transmitted diseases might be described as germs of endearment.

– A political commentator privately told a colleague that lesbians and the 114th Congress have one thing in common—neither does dick.

– While moms celebrate Mother's Day and dads celebrate Father's Day, many teenage boys will celebrate the same holiday many times during the year—Palm Sunday.

– Surprisingly, condoms have something in common with coffins. They're both filled with stiffs, except one's coming and one's going.

– The words "duet yourself" might refer to two people masturbating on their own at the same time.

– Upon hearing that his wife had given birth to quintuplets, a civil rights activist back in 1966 allegedly said, "I have overcome."

– Two patriotic college girls who were touring China were proud that they had their first sexual experiences in the U.S. They wore shirts that read "Made in America".

– A man who had had a few too many drinks loudly propositioned a provocatively-dressed woman in a crowded singles bar and was thrown out by the manager for engaging in aural sex.

– I understand that going out with a castrating female can be a eunuch experience.

– A number of normal, healthy babies have been conceived by artificial insemination, which tends to disprove the old saying: "Spare the rod and spoil the child."

– Upon arriving at his date's apartment for dinner, the insecure man proceeded to tell her a number of stories about his exploits as a great lover. Eventually, the woman said, "Now that we've had our cocktails, it's time for dinner."

– A college girl went to a fraternity beer party, got drunk, spent the night with one of the fraters, and soon after discovered that she was pregnant. After her baby was born, she decided to write a book about her experience, which she entitled *From Beer to Maternity.*

– I understand that in the old days prudent sailors would not make Waves.

– Scientists can always tell if a chromosome is male or female by taking off its genes.

– When the Russians invaded Ukraine, a number of lines from the sixties were revived, such as: "Putin, pull out like your father should have."

– Fewer and fewer women feel comfortable going to the Virgin Islands for their wedding night.

– I met a taxidermist in London who always takes a woman out for a big meal before making love to her. He's used to stuffing a bird before mounting her.

– Men who go out hunting at singles bars like to find women who are game.

– Many years ago I heard about a prudish female elevator operator who was fired from her job because she refused to tell riders that she was going down.

– For a swinging playboy businessman, business is always picking up.

– A man and a woman who were having an ongoing love affair had different lovemaking preferences. He enjoyed wild and passionate sessions, while she preferred slow and gentle intimacy. After dinner at a restaurant one night, the man said to his lady, "My pace or yours?"

– The luckiest hours for men in Paris are between midnight and 4:00 A.M., and are known as "the oui hours of the morning."

– A number of playboys should try out for our Olympic swimming team since they excel in the breast stroke.

– A Vietnam veteran decided to write a book about his combat experiences and the nights he spent with the ladies of the evening in Saigon. His book is entitled *War and Piece.*

– Two college girls arrived back at the dormitory very late on a Saturday night and were interrogated by the dorm supervisor. "Why were you out after hours?" the woman asked. "Because we had to lose two guys who were after ours," the girls replied.

– A male and female lawyer from the same law firm, who were more than just colleagues, went to court one afternoon and ended up without their briefs.

– A woman ran into a man she knew at the theater and unknowingly introduced him to a girlfriend who had once been his lover. The man said, "I think I've already made your acquaintance."

– A single friend of mine was once telling me about one of his many loves. "I used to kiss her lips," he said, "but it's all over now."

– Back in the day, a maternity dress could cause a lot of gossip—but usually not as much as a paternity suit.

– A well-known impersonator surprised his audience by pulling out a wig and doing an impersonation of a celebrity actress he had a crush on for a long time. He told the audience he always wanted to do her.

– A young woman was very frustrated about still being a virgin in her 30's. She was truly fit to be tried.

– Men who make obscene phone calls have sexual hang-ups.

– The interiors of some drive-in movies are quite plush. They have wall-to-wall car petting.

– An elderly virgin might be considered a woman who has not met her maker.

– A farmer's daughter who attends the State Fair for the first time will get herself in a lot of trouble if she cannot keep her calves together.

– A lady saw her bachelor neighbor enter his apartment with an intoxicated woman on his arm. The next day she saw him in the hall and said with a smile, "Who was that girl I saw you outwit last night?"

– When the nightclub comedian had a few drinks and did a striptease on stage, the audience had a chance to watch a comic strip.

– I knew a girl in high school who was as pure as driven snow; however, she has since drifted quite a bit.

– A middle-aged man whose marriage revolves around the kitchen and the bedroom is unhappy because in one place, it's always well done, and in the other place, it's rare.

– A novelty company is coming out with his-and-hers candy underwear. The female version is plain while the male version comes with nuts.

– Most bisexuals do not have strong political convictions. When it comes to voter referendums, they can go either way.

– A photographer once brought his attractive assistant into the darkroom for half an hour to see what would develop.

– Lady Godiva was the biggest gambler of all time. She put everything she had on a horse. While she didn't win, she showed all the way.

– A female English lawyer will have trouble getting a job with an American law firm if she has worked as a solicitor.

– The perfect day for a male attorney is lots of fee mail in the morning and a lot of female in the evening.

– Studies have shown that the most effective form of birth control for a woman is an aural contraceptive—the word "No".

– A man who believed he would require a sex change operation to become a happy, fulfilled person decided to first get some psychiatric help. When the psychiatrist helped the man realize that a sex change was not necessary to solve his problems, the man said, "That's a load off my chest."

– An overweight middle-aged woman was physically attracted to a good-looking young guy and thought she could lure him into an affair with her sex appeal. You might describe the woman as a cock-eyed optimist.

– A prudent guy will always carry condoms with him so they will be available on every conceivable occasion.

– There was an attractive coed at the school I attended who was most accommodating to the guys in my fraternity. Her name was "June," but everyone called her "May."

– There is a company executive who cheats on his wife, drinks heavily, and is a compulsive gambler. His associates unofficially refer to him as "the Vice President."

– Two American law students were touring a museum in London and walked by a medieval chastity belt. One student said to the other, "That must have been the very first antitrust suit."

– The schoolmarm invited an Italian gentleman to her house for dinner. When she asked him what he wanted for dessert, the man put his arm around her and said, "Marmalade."

– A woman who is anxious to conceive and imagines the symptoms of a pregnancy that has not occurred is laboring under a misconception. She also has preconceived notions about parenthood.

– When a thirty-five-year-old woman told her gyne-cologist that she and her husband were thinking about starting a family, the gynecologist told her, 'You'd better get on the stick"

– A high school boy brought his girlfriend and sleeping bag to a secluded spot at an outdoor concert with great expectations. However, the musicians produced the only score of the evening.

– Smoking pot and making love have one basic simi-larity; they're both joint ventures.

– A house where a family with nine children resides could be a house of pill refute.

– After graduating from college, a father took his son aside and said, "I want to give you some advice about sex and real estate and the advice is the same: Get lots while you're young!"

– A smooth-talking playboy persuaded a young lady to take him back to her apartment and then tried to impress her with a philosophical discussion of the hereafter. After a short while, the man began to loosen his tie and said, "Speaking of the hereafter, let me show you what I'm here after."

– I heard rumors that an athletic supporter company and a company that sells body shapers for women will be the new co-sponsors of the TV program "Meet the Press". They want to change the program's name to "Press the Meat".

– I know a woman officer in the army who never takes her meals with the other officers. She likes to mess with the enlisted men.

– A couple of women decided to move from their apartment when the traffic signals at the surrounding intersections froze from the cold. They did not want to live in a red-light district.

– Two teenage boys who were out on a hot double date entered a drive-in after the movie had started. Upon returning to their car from the concession stand during the next showing of the movie, one remarked to the other, "This is where we came in."

– The president of a bank was very concerned when he found out that many of the bank's loans and female employees were overdue.

– Bankers have a hard time understanding why a woman without principle will draw a lot of interest.

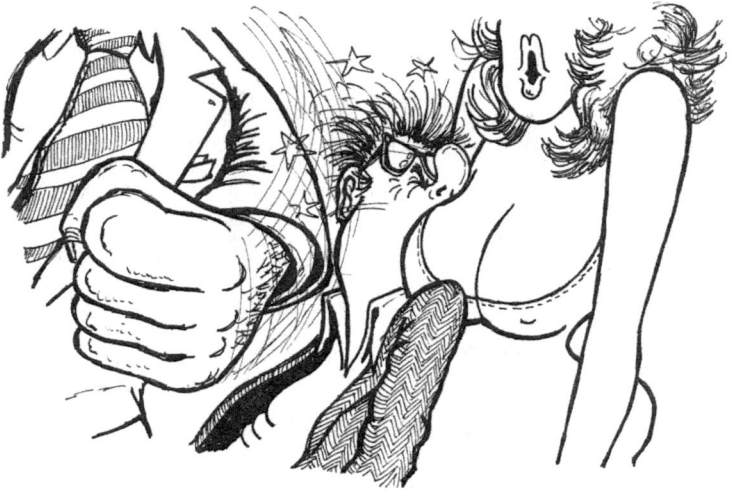

– A short man asked a tall well-endowed model to dance without knowing she was married to a boxer. The man got busted in the mouth.

– A man who was having trouble recalling an important piece of information put his head between his girlfriend's breasts and had her motorboat him. You might say the man was racking his brain trying to remember.

– During World War II, battles between ships on the high seas and sexual intercourse had much in common. They were both naval encounters with the loss of semen.

– A college girl does not have to be an English major to know that "to lay" is the object of a proposition.

– A woman was complaining to her playboy hairdresser about how difficult it was to take care of her long straight hair. Her hairdresser replied with a smile, "Would you like to be bald?"

– In the Garden of Eden, Adam came before Eve—but men usually do.

– Many years ago the male members of the British government could have learned a valuable lesson from the nation's furniture makers—one improper screw can cause an entire cabinet to fall apart.

– A newborn collie was not happy unless he was laying on top of his owner's very large breasts. The best words to describe the dog are "melon collie".

– An e-mail and a penis have one important thing in common. They both can spread a virus.

– An entrepreneur I know believes he does his best creative thinking right before and right after engaging in intercourse. He was always advised to think outside the box.

– A woman who was anxious to become pregnant had her husband make love to her on top of her office's copying machine after hours. She thought it would help her reproduce.

– You might say that men who go to singles bars looking for women are out gal-avanting.

– A woman who likes to monkey around with lots of men might be described as an organ grinder.

– A teenage boy and his friend were watching an adult movie while his parents were away. The movie inspired his friend to try to reach climax on his own. When the boy's parents came home earlier than expected and his father saw what his friend was doing, he said, "Where do you get off masturbating in my house?

– After having a few drinks, a man came up to a woman at a singles' bar and said, "I'd tell you a joke about my penis, but it's too long", to which the woman replied, "I'd tell you a joke about my vagina, but you won't get it."

– Members of a college fraternity built a raft and floated down the local river with their rear ends exposed. Allegedly, the incident was the inspiration for the song "Moon River."

THE END—TIME TO BUTT OUT

TECHNIQUES FOR PUNSTERS

If the reader has had the endurance to become familiar with the collection of puns in the first part of the book, he or she is now ready to develop the punning techniques which I believe separate a true artist from a person who can occasionally rattle off a pun when he or she hears a familiar word. Discussed below are a few basic techniques and a few secondary techniques, which will guide a punster in developing the ability to blend clever puns smoothly into normal conversation.

First of all, and of utmost importance, a punster who is verbally interacting with other people should only use puns that make sense in the context of that inter-action. The mere fact that he knows a pun on a word that comes up in the conversation or which is brought to mind by the situation does not mean he should use it at that time unless it reasonably fits in with what is being discussed or what is happening. A punster should strive to make his puns with a perfectly straight face, in a normal tone of voice, so that they are consistent with the rest of the conversation. When a pun is told in this manner, it is not unusual for at least one person in the group not to know what hit him until someone groans it to his attention. (If no one in the group catches the pun, be sure to stop the conversation, smile, and tell everyone what a great play on words they just missed!)

The following are some illustrations of the first technique from my personal experiences. One night during my college days I was at a restaurant in St. Louis with some friends. We finished our main course, and I asked the waitress for the dessert menu. She replied that the only dessert left that night was rice pudding. I instantaneously responded in a disbelieving tone of voice, "You're putting me on."

A couple of years ago at my old law firm I went to see the bookkeeper about getting reimbursed for some cab fares and other business expenses I had paid for out of my own money. She took out a pad of petty cash slips and had me fill out a couple. When I finished, she said, "Why don't you keep the rest of the pad for future use," to which I replied, "Great! I've always wanted a pad of my own."

Recently, I was in Kansas City on behalf of one of my clients, trying to arrange new mortgage financing for a small shopping center. While driving down a major commercial highway, one of the mortgage bankers I was with said, "Look at all the doughnut shops that are going out of business," to which I immediately replied, "Apparently, they're running out of dough."

Finally, during the last football season I was very much involved in watching the playoff games on TV while my wife was wrapping Christmas gifts. She commented that she needed some ribbon for the gifts, and I promised to go out and get some at the end of the game, in about a half hour. After over an hour had passed, and the game was not over, she said something like, "I'm sure glad I have all this ribbon to wrap the presents," to which I shouted, "Quit ribbing me!"

On all of the above occasions I came up with puns that made sense in light of the remarks directed at me, and which were logical continuations of the ongoing conversations. The puns made in these situations should be contrasted with the following puns which were made by other persons in my presence: "I can't bear the thought" (by a bear exhibit at the local zoo), "That's a lot of bull" (upon seeing a bull from a car on a country road), and "Something fishy is going on here" (upon catching a fish on a Wisconsin lake). When the above puns were made, the amateur punsters involved were merely reciting puns on easily pun-able words without regard to the context of the situation; the puns were not meaningful in light of what was happening at the time, nor were they a response to something said or done by another person. An accomplished punster would not have impugned his honor with those puns.

My second technique, which potentially could be the most useful and productive, is utilized in situations where a punster thinks of or is reminded of a good pun he would like to make, but feels he cannot smoothly fit it into the ongoing conversation. In these situations a punster should create tangential conversation or concoct a plausible story that will enable him to make his pun effectively. The created conversation should flow smoothly from and be a reasonably logical extension of the ongoing conversation, and again, should be done in normal tone of voice with a perfectly straight face.

A couple of examples will help illustrate this technique. Some time ago there was a popular discount department store chain in the Chicagoland area called "Shopper's World." One time I was involved in a conversation in which someone was discussing the unpleasantness of her last visit to the dentist. I subsequently went off on a tangent that went something like this: "Speaking of dentists, I just read in the paper yesterday that they are planning to open a huge dental office on the Near North Side with chairs for twenty-five dentists. I think they plan to call the office 'Chopper's World'."

On another occasion, I was with a group of people who were talking about their respective vacations in Europe. When it was my turn, I made up the following story: "Of all the countries in Europe, I had the best time in Finland. That's probably because I speak the language." Someone in the group then said, "You speak Finnish?" I replied, "That's right. However, I must admit that my Finnish isn't too good; but, neither is my beginning."

On a third occasion, I was coming back to my law office after lunch when the receptionist announced, "Your wife just called" to which I replied, "Which one?" A senior partner who was standing nearby looked at me disdainfully and sniffed, "You have more than one?" I replied: "Yes, and its bigamy to admit it."

In all of the above situations I manipulated and altered the direction of the conversation to give myself the opportunity to slip in one of my favorite puns. My audience was not aware that my stories were complete fabrications until I lowered the boom on them. It takes years of dedicated practice to be convincing in setting up a pun in this manner without letting people know that you are not for real.

A variation on my second technique, which has given me a great deal of mileage, is picking up a newspaper or magazine and pretending to read (or summarize) some fictitious event. One time at my in-laws' house I picked up the Sunday paper, pretended to be looking at a specific news account, and said the following: "Did you see this article about the terrorists in Nicaragua?" My in-laws indicated they had not. "They tried to kill one of their political opponents, a matador, by planting a bomb in the stomach of one of the bulls in the ring. The whole situation is becoming abominable."

The third basic technique is often invoked when a punster really has to stretch the words in his pun or when the pun he plans to use is a little on the obvious side. Also, this technique can be used when the punster is not sure whether or not he has already perpetrated the pun he has in mind on the people he's with. In all these circumstances, the thing to do is to make the pun by blaming it on someone else.

I have three favorite ways of putting the blame on someone else, which once again can best be illustrated by a few examples. If the subject of Moors comes up in a discussion of history or culture, you might look at the person you're talking to at an appropriate point in the conversation and say with an acknowledging nod of the head, "I know what you're thinking: the Moor the merrier." Alternately, if you happened to be discussing great artistic painters, you might turn to someone with a grimacing look at some opportune moment and accusingly say, "You're probably going to say something like 'Easel come, easel go.' "As another possibility, when the time is right and you are talking about oil with the ideal prospective victim, you can simply say with a look of anguish, "I know. The oily bird gets the worm."

In essence, the third technique is a useful device for the times a punster is a little embarrassed or inhibited about making a particular pun, and a suitable scapegoat is present. In addition, this technique affords one the unique opportunity of being a punster at the same time he or she is pretending to react like one of the unfortunate victims.

It should be pointed out at this time that there are occasions when the people you are with really do inadvertently make puns. As the enlightened punster, you have the option of either pointing out and complimenting the person on his pun, or letting him know about it with a look and words of anguish, depending on who the unenlightened punster is and the circumstances involved. I recall one particular lecture in my commercial law class at Northwestern University when our professor was discussing a particular case dealing with a swimming pool company. During the discussion, the professor made comments about how the business had "liquidity" problems that eventually forced the owner "to go under," and when the bank that had loaned him money took over, they were anxious to "wash their hands of the business". Considering who was involved and the circumstances, I definitely felt it was in my best interests to compliment the professor on his subtle punmanship.

When the circumstances that would occasion the use of my third technique exist, but it might be difficult or awkward to imply that a particular pun is on someone else's mind, a punster should use my fourth basic technique. The fourth technique is actually a tactful way of coping with the moments of weakness that every punster occasionally has when he feels that he absolutely has to make a certain pun or his mind will not be at ease. If you are the punster when these circumstances occur, the following approach should be taken. At some appropriate point in the conversation, you should make your pun in a very deliberate manner by giving the impression that everyone knows the pun should be said, and it might as well be you who gets the job done. For instance, if the subject again happens to be oil (and assuming you have the courage), you could use expressions like, ''you know the old saying-'Oil's fair in love and war,' "or, ''you know what they always say—'Oil's well that ends well.'" It should be pointed out, however, that even when this technique and the third one are used, the puns must be reasonably consistent with the context of the conversation and situation, lest the punster lower himself to the level of a mere amateur.

Initially, a punster is likely to use the basic techniques discussed above with adaptable puns he or she has absorbed and stored in his or her mind for future reference. Eventually, however, he or she should start to think like a veteran punster and develop the ability to create new puns spontaneously while involved in ordinary conversation.

In addition to my basic techniques, there are a few secondary techniques which can be used by a person who has already started to think like a seasoned punster and whose ears are attuned to hearing pun-able words. The secondary techniques are more limited in applicability because their use is more dependent on the specific words of others. Nevertheless, these methods of punning have been used most effectively by some well-known people in the world of comedy, and can offer a talented punster additional excellent ways of PUNishing his victims.

There are occasions when someone will say a word that reminds you of a similar-sounding word. In these situations the punster can pretend that he did not hear what the person said, and inquire whether the person said the word the punster is thinking of. A couple of examples again will best illustrate this technique.

A number of years ago my younger brother Marc came home from a barber shop in Winnetka, Illinois, and my grandfather Jake said to him, "Say, that's a nice haircut. Where did you get it?" My brother replied, "At Smales," to which my grandfather responded, "What! You say it smells?"

There was also the time at one of my summer jobs during college when my supervisor and I were discussing a cost-benefit study we were planning to make for a new highway project. My supervisor said something like, "I have very distinct ideas about how to structure this study," to which I quickly responded with an inquisitive look, "you say your ideas stink?" It so happens that I was not rehired by that company the following summer.

If you are to use this type of punning, the people you are with must cooperate by saying the right words; also you must have sharp ears and enough punning experience to recognize special words which can spontaneously be turned into questioning puns. Groucho Marx made extremely humorous use of this method of punning on his *You Bet Your Life* show.

Closely related to the above technique are the corollary techniques of responding to a pun-able word said by another person by knowingly continuing the conversation in a direction not intended by the victim (until you pretend to acknowledge your misunderstanding at some point), or by physically reacting to what is said in a manner not anticipated by the victim. Again, a few personal experiences can best demonstrate what I have in mind.

A few years ago, I was shopping for some furniture for my apartment with my girlfriend. At one store, I was talking to a salesman about end tables. The salesman looked at one particular table, which was situated next to my girlfriend, and said, "There's a real beauty. Just look at those legs." I continued to look in the direction of the table and my girlfriend and said something like this, "yes, those are great legs. And look at the rest of that body, and those sexy eyes." I slowly turned toward the salesman's puzzled face, hesitated, and then said with a look of sudden enlightenment, "Oh! You mean the table! I thought you meant the young lady." The salesman managed to fake a faint smile and a slight laugh, and politely suggested that I look around the store on my own for a while.

When I first started working for a law firm, a secretary in the firm and I had a discussion about the work habits of the various lawyers in the office. At one point in the discussion she was talking about how sloppy and disorganized the senior partner's office was, referring to the ever-present foot-high layer of papers on his desk She subsequently asked me if I kept my drawers neat, to which I replied, "Oh, yes. My wife irons and folds every pair." After hearing her snicker a few seconds later, I pretended to see the light by saying, "Oh you mean my desk drawers. Yeah, they're pretty neat."

Turning to the second variation, I recall the time a number of months ago when my wife and I were having dinner at a well-known restaurant in Chicago. My wife had ordered trout and I had ordered roast duck. The waiter brought out my wife's dinner and a short time later the captain came out of the kitchen with my roast duck. He approached our table and said in a questioning tone, "Duck?" I instantly ducked my head beneath the table (with my arm over my head), to the total bafflement of the captain, the embarrassment of my wife, and the amusement of the couple at the next table. After the captain stood in silence for a few seconds, my wife said to him, 'Yes, he ordered duck," at which point the man put my dinner down with a slight, forced smile and left. It so happened that upon leaving the restaurant, instead of hearing the usual "Good night, please come again," all we heard was "Good night." The Marx Brothers made excellent use of this form of punmanship in their many movies.

As a final example of the above two corollary techniques, I recall a very recent incident which demonstrates how the two methods of punning can be combined effectively. My wife and I went to a restaurant in a nearby suburb with my cousin Harley. As we walked in the door, the hostess came up to greet us and said to my cousin, "Check your coat?" Harley immediately proceeded to examine every inch of his coat from top to bottom, then turned to the bewildered hostess and said, "Looks okay to me." The great Mel Brooks has hilariously combined the two techniques and used each separately in his recent movies and personal interviews.

As with the mishearing technique initially discussed, the misunderstanding and physical reaction techniques require the victim to provide the punster with the right words to play off, and the punster must be able to react spontaneously. These two methods of punning are especially suited to those readers with a flair for the dramatic.

When the reader has thoroughly familiarized himself with a number of the puns in the first part of the book and understands the punning techniques outlined above, he is ready to be unleashed upon the public. Hopefully, the categorical collection and the suggested techniques will serve as a training manual until the art becomes second nature.

Visit

www.kingofpuns.com

for more information about the Author and his books.